SOLOS

FOR

STRINGS

AN INDISPENSABLE STRING INSTRUMENT COLLECTION FOR SOLO OR SECTIONAL UNISON PLAYING.

COMPILED AND ARRANGED BY

Harvey S. Whistler

FOR

VIOLIN SOLO (First Position)   CELLO SOLO (First Position)

VIOLA SOLO (First Position)   STRING BASS SOLO (First & Second Positions)

PIANO ACCOMPANIMENT

★

RUBANK

HAL•LEONARD CORPORATION

7777 W. BLUEMOUND RD. P.O. BOX 13819 MILWAUKEE, WI 53213

PREFACE

SOLOS FOR STRINGS represents an indispensable collection of famous compositions, styled in easy arrangements for solo playing on the violin, viola, cello and string bass, all with Piano Accompaniment. The material presented is admirably suited for players with only a limited amount of technic, or for those who have only studied their respective instruments a short length of time. The collection may be advantageously utilized as **SUPPLEMENTARY MATERIAL** to accompany **ANY** class or individual method, and is so arranged that it may be used equally well in either homogeneous or heterogeneous groupings of stringed instruments.

Students should have no difficulty in playing **SOLOS FOR STRINGS** after just a few months of study, and progressive music educators of the public schools will find it convenient to draw upon the materials of this collection for student recitals presented at the end of the first or second semester of school as a culmination of the work of the elementary string class.

Heretofore, the lack of easy music for such instruments in particular as the viola, cello and string bass, has been a factor in limiting the possibilites of solo performances by students studying these instruments. However, with the advent of **SOLOS FOR STRINGS**, a definite step forward has been taken educationally by providing materials that will fill a long-felt need and which will not only enhance the value of the elementary stages of string class study, but will also increase its scope and vitalize its possibilities.

All of the solos used in this collection have been carefully bowed and edited, with particular attention being focused on scoring each solo in an idiom characteristic of the instrument for which it was being arranged.

It is to the thousands of string players in the schools of America, that this collection of **SOLOS FOR STRINGS** is respectfully dedicated.

Harvey S. Whistler

Piano Accompaniment ①

LARGO
from
NEW WORLD SYMPHONY

To be played in a smooth, sustained manner. The bow
should at all times be drawn parallel with the bridge
and not be allowed to slide back and forth between the
bridge and fingerboard.

DVORAK
Arr. by Harvey S Whistler

MERRY WIDOW WALTZ

To be played in an elegant, graceful manner. The fingers of the left hand should at all times be placed firmly on the strings they are stopping, while the bow passes evenly and lightly from one string to another.

FRANZ LEHAR
Arr. by Harvey S. Whistler

Tempo di Valse

(9) Elegante

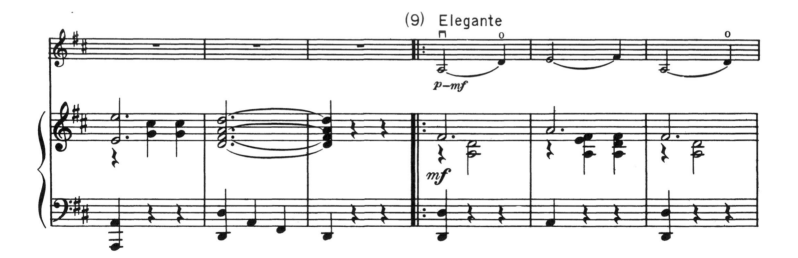

(13-45)   (17-49)

(21-53)

(25-57) (29-61)

(33-65)

(37-69)

Piano Accompaniment ③

MELODY IN F

To be played in a fervent, ardent manner.   A singing
tone should be maintained througout the number. The
bowing should be broad and connected with changes
from down bow to up bow and up bow to down bow made
as quietly as possible with little or no break in the con-
tinuity of tone.

RUBENSTEIN
Arr. by Harvey S. Whistler

Piano Accompaniment ④

VOLGA BOATMAN

To be played in a plaintive, mournful manner. All dynamic
markings should be very carefully observed, and the sad,
melancholy character of this piece, representing as it does,
the utter hopelessness and misery in the lives of the Volga
Boatmen, be expressively brought out in playing it.

RUSSIAN FOLK SONG
Arr. by Harvey S. Whistler

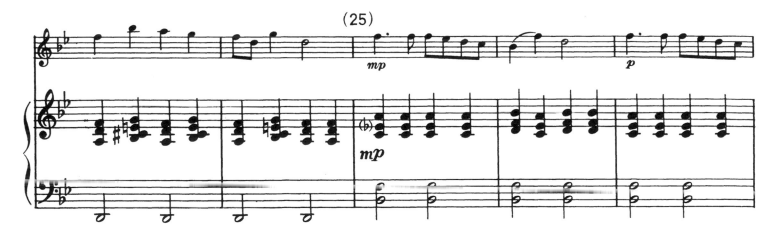

Piano Accompaniment ⑤

BARCAROLLE
from
TALES OF HOFFMANN

To be played in a calm, easy manner. The tone should
be flowing, with a touch of expressive beauty. At no
time should the tempo be hurried.

OFFENBACH
Arr. by Harvey S. Whistler

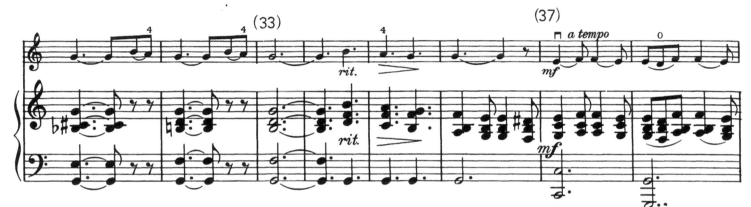

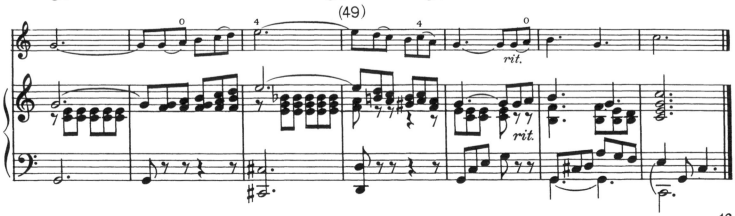

13

ANDANTINO

To be played in a tender, endearing manner. The tone
should be that of unaffected grace and charm. A sup-
pleness of bowing should be brought into play in order
that this captivating theme may stand out as one smooth,
unbroken line of melody.

LEMARE
Arr. by Harvey S. Whistler

DRINK TO ME ONLY WITH THINE EYES

To be played in a noble, dignified manner. The tone should
be one of clearness and purity, so necessary in portray-
ing the spirit of old English ballads of this nature.

OLD ENGLISH BALLAD
Arr. by Harvey S. Whistler

SWANEE RIVER

To be played in a simple, unadorned manner. The tone should begin distinctly and remain free and unhampered throughout this most beloved of all American compositions.

STEPHEN C. FOSTER
Arr. by Harvey S. Whistler

Andante e semplice

Con fervore
(5)

(9)

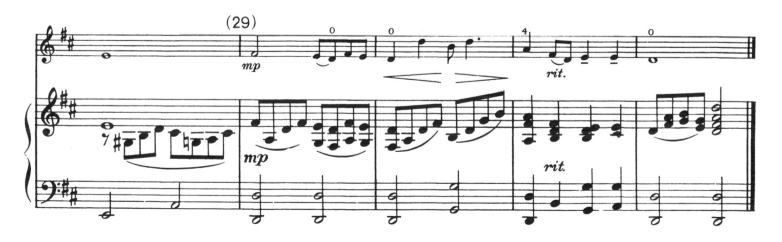

LIEBESTRAUME

To be played in an expressive, emotional manner. Prime importance should be placed on bringing out the pathos and sentiment demanded by this dream of love. The player should "breathe a soul" into this work.

LISZT
Arr. by Harvey S. Whistler

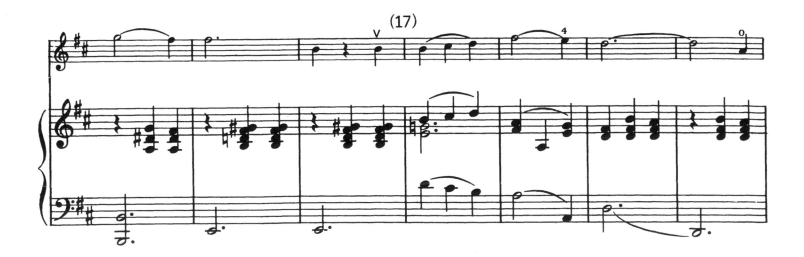

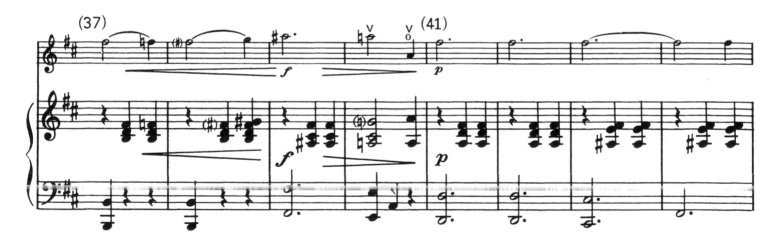

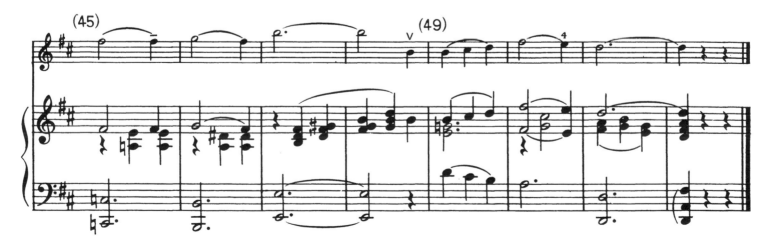

Piano Accompaniment ⑩

EVENING STAR

from

TANNHAUSER

To be played in a sublime, exalted manner. A poetic tone of delicate nuance should be employed to bring out the consummate genius of the great Wagner, which crystalizes in this appealing love melody, demanding as it does, a lofty interpretation.

WAGNER
Arr. by Harvey S. Whistler

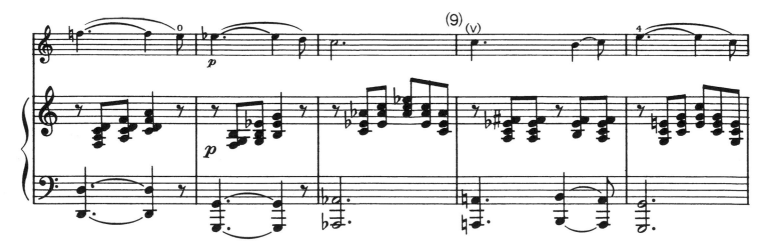

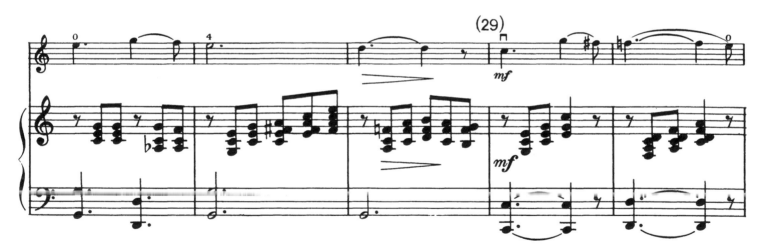

⑪

NOCTURNE

To be played in a polished, refined manner. The tone should
be one of vibrant quality, with extreme care given to see-
ing that the tempo at all times remains steady.

VON BLON
Arr. by Harvey S. Whistler

Moderato

(5) Elegante

Copyright MCMXL by Rubank, Inc., Chicago, Ill.
International Copyright Secured

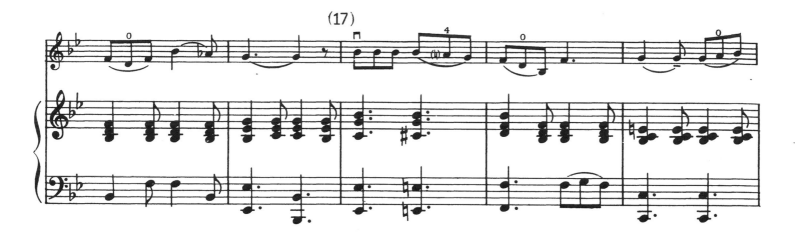

ANDANTE
from
FIFTH SYMPHONY

To be played in a dreamy, exotic manner. The romantic stamp of this haunting melody is best expressed in a mood removed from worldly tought. Strict attention should be paid to the bowing which has been carefully marked.

TSCHAIKOWSKY
Arr. by Harvey S. Whistler

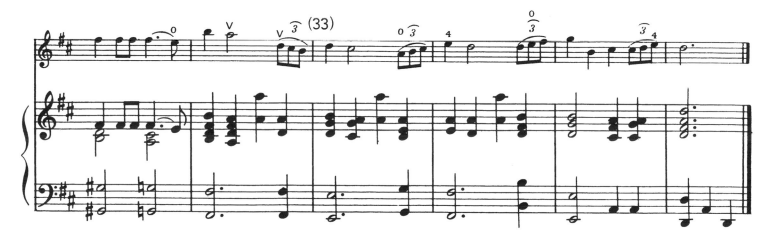